AF205258

For Sir Sven Wahlroos (in memoriam)
- who inspired me, who enlightened me,
who helped me find myself -

Gedichte & Geschichten
und andere so Sachen

Poems & Stories
and other such things

Die Deutsche Nationalbibliothek verzeichnet diese Publikation in der
Deutschen Nationalbibliografie; detaillierte bibliografische Daten sind im Internet
über http://www.dnb.de abrufbar.

Erste Auflage 2018 / First Edition 2018
Copyright © Ulrich Krentz

Alle Rechte vorbehalten / All rights reserved

Der Inhalt dieses Buches und sein Titel sind urheberrechtlich geschützt.
The content of this book and its title are protected by copyright.

Jeder Nachdruck, jede Wiedergabe, Übersetzung, Vervielfältigung und Verbreitung, auch
von Teilen des Werkes oder von Abbildungen, jede Abschrift, auch auf fotomechanischem
Wege oder im Magnettonverfahren, im Vortrag, Funk, Fernsehen, Internet, Telefonüber-
tragung sowie Speicherung in Datenaufbereitungsanlagen, bedarf der Genehmigung des
Autors.
Umschlagentwurf / Cover Design, Michael McLynskey, Luxembourg
Buchblock/book block/Layout, Apfelgrafik & Design, Trier, Germany
Bilder und Fotos aus eigener Sammlung / Pictures and photos by own collection and
iStockphoto: Seiten/pages: 14, 20, 24, 60, 100, 102, 112
Shutterstock: Seiten/pages: 28, 32, 34, 36, 38, 40, 48, 74, 88, 92, 106, 108, 110, 114, 134
Harald Meierjohann: Seiten/pages 18, 30
Korrektorat Deutsch: Klaus-Ulrich Wolpert, Luxemburg
Copy-editing/proofreading English: Graham Chambers, Portugal
Herstellung und Verlag: Books on Demand GmbH, Norderstedt, Germany
Gesetzt in 10pt Garamond (Claude Garamond, * 1499 - † 1561, Typograph)

ISBN: 9783746006598

„Wenn alles andere scheitert, schreib was dein Herz dir sagt. Du kannst dich nicht auf deine Augen verlassen, wenn deine Vorstellungen unscharf sind."

Mark Twain

❦

"When all else fails, write what your heart tells you. You can't depend on your eyes when your imagination is out of focus."

Mark Twain

Inhaltsverzeichnis / Content

Ende / The End

Vorwort

Nachtgedanken, sie fliegen mir zu, sie kommen verkleidet im Traume! Der Morgen kommt, weckt mich mit seinem Lichte und seinen Geräuschen, ich greife mir die Wort- und Textfragmente der verrauschten Nacht und schreibe auf was mir von ihnen geblieben. Wörter und ihre Gebilde finde ich wieder, teils im Englischen und teils im Deutschen, wie versteckt in Schubladen eines alten, geheimnisvollen chinesischen Apothekerschränkchens. Ich mische zusammen, was zusammen zu gehören scheint. Ich arbeite an dem mir verbliebenen. Die Sprache hierbei scheint willkürlich, zumindest dort, wo ich diese beherrsche. Texte sind in Englisch, Texte sind in Deutsch und gelegentlich auch mal in beiden. Ich bitte den Leser um Nachsicht!

...

Prologue

"Night thoughts", they just come to me, all clothed in dreams! The morning comes, wakes me with its lights and sounds, I seize the words and text fragments of the faded night and write down what has remained. Words and their constructions reappear in English and in German, as if hidden in the drawers of an old Chinese medicine cabinet full of secrets. I blend what seems to belong together. I work on what is left to me. The language seems arbitrary, - where I master the language that is. Text is in English, text is in German and occasionally in the two. I do beg the reader's forbearance!

Über die Zeiten / About the Seasons

Wunder der Natur

Und ist der Tag dann fast zu Ende,
Find ich die Zeit spazieren zu gehen,
Tausch' dann die kalten weißen Wände,
Um die Farben der Natur zu sehen.

Das ist mein tägliches Entfliehen
Vor schaler Luft und engem Raum,
Weiß doch die Umwelt nur geliehen,
Erleb sie täglich wie ein Traum!

So streich ich abends durch die Felder
Und lausch dem Wind im Korne zu.
Wie Burgen scheinen mir die Wälder,
Hier findet alle Eile ruh!

Des Nachts der Mond durchs Fenster strahlt,
Zieht ganz silbern seine Spur
Und so mir schönste Schatten malt,
Das ist das Wunder der Natur!

Trier, August 2015

The Storms of Spring

The storms of spring are blowing,
Impatiently they scream
With gusts so deadly growing,
Whole trees now block the stream
Debris is flying through the air,
The birds are found in hiding,
As every creature seeks some lair,
In shelter safe abiding!

Trier, March 2010

GEDICHTE & GESCHICHTEN / POEMS & STORIES

Es ist Frühling, Frühling ists!

Über Nacht ist er gekommen,
Mit all seinen Symbolen und Attributen,
Hat sich die Farben zurückgewonnen;
Blumenzwiebeln, die lang geduldig ruhten,
Bunt sprießen, in goldenem Scheine sich sonnen.

Noch ist kein Winter je geblieben,
Mit heiteren Gedanken wollen wir uns belohnen;
Des Schnees Weiß scheint in die Maiglöckchen vertrieben,
Altvertraute Düfte wieder in unseren Nasen wohnen.

Was fast schon vergessen, ist wieder entdeckt,
Das Leben im Drinnen ist nun auch im Draußen,
In gefrorenen Mündern das Lachen geweckt!

Luxemburg/Trier, März 2017

GEDICHTE & GESCHICHTEN / POEMS & STORIES

Frühling (jetzt ist es Zeit)

Herr, es ist Zeit. Der Winter war sehr groß!
Nimm deinen Schatten von den Sonnenuhren,
Und auf die Felder lass die Pflüge los!

Hauch den prallen Knospen neu deine Kräfte ein;
Gib ihnen jetzt nur die südlicheren Tage,
Dränge sie zur Vollendung hin, und jage
Des Frühjahrs Wärme in die Blüten rein.

Jetzt ist die Zeit, um sich was Neues aufzubauen.
Wer bislang allein war, sollte es nicht mehr bleiben,
Sollte träumen, lesen und wieder Briefe schreiben
Und nach neuen alten Freunden schauen;
Gemeinsam in den Straßen, den Winter vertreiben!

Trier/Luxemburg, nach R. M. Rilke

Bernsteinsonne

Golden scheint der Kerzen Licht
Durch mein bleiern kristallenes Glas,
Sich immer wieder brechend
In der bernsteinfarbenen Farbe meines alten Malz Whiskys,
Mich an die Morgensonne eines frühen Sommertages erinnernd!

Trier, Dezember 2016

...

Amber sunrise

Gold shines the candlelight
Through the leaded crystal,
Multiply reflecting
In my old, single malt,
Like an early summer's morning sun!

Trier, December 2016

Sommer (Loblied auf den Herbst)

Wenn ich denn dann des Sommers heiße Tage
Mir eintauschen muss mit der,
Wenn auch selbstgewählten,
Doch kühlenden Dunkelheit des Raumes,
Dann sehne ich mir her,
Ganz erwartungsvoll,
Den Meister Herbst mit seinen Kräften!

Trier, Juli 2015

...

Summer (Ode to Autumn)

When finally I must exchange summer's hot days
For my self-chosen,
Yet cooling comfort of the dark,
With expectation I long for
Lord Autumn and his powers!

Trier, July 2015

Sommerregen

Der Regen an die Fenster klopft
- Ich laß' ihn nicht herein -
Ich seh' an den Scheiben, wie es tropft -
Das trocknet bald der Sonnenschein!

Douglas, Isle of Man, September 2017

Morgensonne

Durchs Fenster die Sonne leuchtet mir am frühen Morgen
Und färbt sie bunt, meine noch verschlafenen Gedanken.
Hebt ganz langsam den Nebel vergangener Träume Sorgen;
Ach, wie gern würd' ich mich doch bei ihr bedanken!

Luxemburg, Januar 2018

Spätsommer

Und schon schmecken die Abende wieder nach Herbst,
Wenig noch ist von Sommers Odem in der Luft verblieben.
Der Sonne Strahlen kitzeln nur mehr halbherzig die Flure
Mit langen Schatten, überall, als Boten ihres späten Lichts!

Trier, August 2017

...

Late Summer

And now the evenings taste of autumn
The air devoid of summer's breath
Half-hearted beams caress the meadows
Heralds of their coming death!

Trier, August 2017 (translated by Graham Chambers)

Herbst

Vom Wind befreite Kronen
Voller bunter Blätter – als totes Laub – der Boden,
Glitzernd getupft mit den Tropfen des frischen Regens
Scheinen wie die Tränen des vergangenen Sommers.

Luxemburg, November 2013

Melancholia

In dieser dunklen Jahreszeit
Machen sich Gedanken breit;
Es ist der flackernde Kerzenschein
Der das Sonnenlicht ersetzt;
Lange Schatten auf der Erde
Und dunkle unter den Augen.

Wie gefangen in der Enge einer Zwangsjacke,
Geschnürt von den zu kurzen Tagen,
Auf den Frühling wartend
Und den Knoten lösend!

Detmold/Trier, Mai 2016

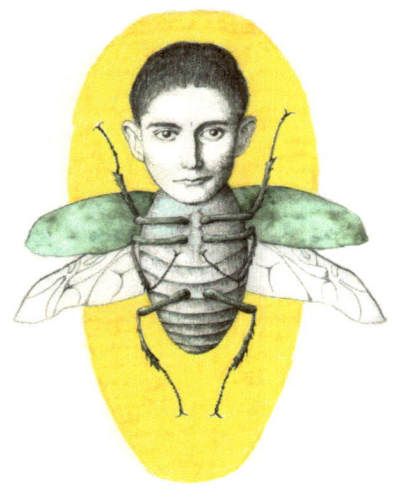

Anfang

Schon wieder ist ein Jahr vergangen
Und so viel in diesem ist geschehen,
Von Änderungen noch ganz befangen
Kann ich so manches kaum verstehen.

Die Zeit der Lichter ist gekommen,
Leckere Düfte ziehen durch die Stadt,
Vom Treiben rundherum benommen
Seh' ich mich an den Menschen satt.

Lautes Rufen, schallendes Lachen,
Ein jeder gern vergisst die Zeit,
Lässt neue Geister wiedererwachen;
Vergessen ist so manches Leid!

Der Morgen scheint in weiter Ferne
Und nur das Jetzt ist mir nah genug.
Hielt ich die Zeit an doch so gerne
Und weiß doch selbst, es wär' nur Trug!

Die langen Nächte noch länger scheinen,
Mit Büchern, dicker als denn je,
Find ich mich wieder in alten Reimen
Bevor ich schließlich schlafen geh.

Und dann erlebe ich im Traume
Was am Tag mir kaum gelingt;
Bin wie Samsa in lichtem Raume
Der seinen Panzer doch bezwingt!

Luxemburg, Oktober 2014

Wintersonnenwende

Scheinbar zögerlich nur traut sich des Morgens erster Sonnenschein durch
meine Fenster,
Als wenn er Winters Dunkelheit zu fürchten hätte.
Nur selten streifen der Sonne Strahlen diese Tage das Innere meines Raumes
- Kaum mehr als ein Funkeln -
Das von Lichtes Fluten des Sommers nur schwer träumen lässt.

Trier/Luxemburg, Winter 2016

...

Winter solstice

Morning's first sunlight waits at my window,
As if afraid of winter dark.
Rarely does he come inside these days
- Hardly more than a spark -
Making it hard to dream of summer's flooding light.

Trier/Luxembourg, Winter 2016

Schneeflocke

Eine Schneeflocke entsteht,
Wenn sich in den Wolken
Bei unter 12 °C, feinste Tröpfchen unterkühlten Wassers um
Z.B. Staubteilchen bilden, und an diesen gefrieren.
Die so entstandenen Eiskristalle fallen,
Zunehmend an Gewicht gewinnend,
Schließlich nach unten auf die Erde.

Die Farbe Weiß ist für uns Menschen ein Farbeindruck,
Der entsteht, wenn ein Material das Licht remittiert,
Dass die drei Zapfen der Netzhaut gleichmäßig
Und mit hoher Intensität gereizt werden.
Der Farbreiz für unser Wahrnehmen von Weiß besteht also darin,
Dass alle drei Farbvalenzen gleich sind.

Luxemburg, Winter 2015

...

Snowflake

A snowflake is created,
When in the clouds,
At minus 12 degrees, fine droplets of super-cooled water
Accrete on particles of dust, and freeze.
The resulting crystals of ice
Fall, increasing their weight, finally down to earth.

The colour white is for us humans an impression
That occurs when material reflects light
Which stimulates the three cones of the retina equally
And with high intensity.
The stimulus for our perception of white, therefore, is
That all three valences of colour are equal.

Luxembourg, Winter 2015

**Christmas
In the City**

Wow, it's Christmas again,
The time those little brats squash
Their cold little fingers in sticky woolly mittens
And their little greasy noses against toyshop windows.

The smells of sausage in rancid fat
Travelling through the overcrowded streets
With one drunk old Santa in his worn out costume
Accompanied by slurring voices of too much mulled wine.

The off tune choir
Competing with the
Church bells' tolls
And an abandoned
Plucked fir tree
Calling for mercy!

MERRY CHRISTMAS!

Trier/Luxembourg, Christmas 2014

Fata Morgana? (Weihnacht in der Wüste)

Das Salz der Erde ist der Schnee meiner Wüste.
Hier, wo alles verloren scheint,
Kommt doch alles wieder zusammen!
Es ist hier, wo das Licht der Dämmerung sich zärtlich-funkelnd reflektiert,
Wie gefallene Sterne vom Himmel in der Wüsten Schnee.

„Immerhin mich wird umgeben
Gottes Himmel, dort wie hier,
Und als Totenlampen schweben
Nachts die Sterne über mir." *

Die bleibende Wärme des späten Tages schafft einen surrealen Augenblick
Einer nicht wirklichen Kälte, in einer viel zu wirklichen Hitze, nur

„Es macht die Wüste schön," sagte der kleine Prinz, „dass sie irgendwo (immer)
*einen Brunnen birgt."**

Wie ein einst in "Der kleiner Prinz"* nur ganz kopfüber und…
…Falls es einen Himmel auf Erden gibt, wäre er wohl hier!

Luxemburg/Trier, September/Oktober/November 2014
*Heinrich Heine und Antoine de Saint-Exupéry

Fata Morgana? (Christmas in the Desert)

The salt of the earth is the snow of my desert.
Here, where everything seems lost,
Everything comes together!
It is here, where the twilight gently reflects glitteringly,
Like stars fallen from heaven,
The desert snow.

"Tis no matter! For God's heaven
Will be round me, there as here,
And the stars that swing at even,
*Will be lamps above my bier."**

The remaining warmth of The Late Day creates a most surreal moment
Of one non-existing cold, into a too existing heat, only

"What makes the desert beautiful," says the little prince "is that somewhere
*it hides (always) a well."**

Feeling like once "The little Prince"* all upside down and...
...If there is a Heaven on Earth, it would be all here!

Luxembourg/Trier, September/October/November 2014
*Heinrich Heine and Antoine de Saint-Exupéry

Über Menschen / About People

Mensch, Vater!

Nach frühen Jahren in verlorenen Zeiten
Und in der Hölle fast erfroren,
Aus ewigen Märschen und kalten Weiten
Hast Du Dich selber neu geboren!

Mit wachem Blick und ohne Klagen,
Keine Arbeit schien Dir je zu schwer,
So manchen Schmerz ganz still ertragen,
Kam doch die neue Zeit daher!

Aus den Erinnerungen Deiner Jugend
Hast Du schöneren Träumen nachgestrebt
Und mit Bescheidenheit als größte Tugend
Würdig Deine Zeit gelebt!

Die Zeit ist Dir nicht stehen geblieben,
Hat so viel Gutes noch gebracht,
Den Stolz Dir ins Gesicht geschrieben,
Wie das Leben es nur macht!

Ganz langsam schloss Dein Vorhang sich,
Warf seine Schatten schon zu lang
Und war nie ein Weg zu weit für Dich,
Kam schließlich doch Dein letzter Gang!

Luxemburg/Trier, Januar/Februar 2013

Tisch im Baum

Geschaffen von Tischlers Meisterhand
Ist der Tisch an dem ich täglich sitze;
Esse und trinke, erzähle und lausche, lache und weine,
Mit der Kraft des Baumes in dessen Stamm gewachsen
- Im ewigen Kampf gegen der Erden magnetische Kräfte -
Kommt er mir entgegen,
Mir, der ich an ihm doch aufrecht sitzen darf!

August 2014, Luxemburg

Zum Gedenken an meinen Großvater Heinrich Hofmeister

...

Table in Tree

Made by master craftsman's hand
Is the table where every day I sit
Eat and drink, talk and listen, laugh and cry
By the strength of the tree from whose bole it is made
-in the eternal fight against Earth's magnetic powers-
It comes towards me...
Me, who dare sit at it upright!

August 2014, Luxembourg

In Memory of my Grandfather Heinrich Hofmeister

Frühstück mit Onkel Hermann

So sitz ich heut' nun hier an Deinem Grab
- Zu erzählen hätt' ich dir doch so viel -
Dir, der viel zu früh sein Leben gab,
Für Feldmarschall und Kaiser fiel,
Für deutschen Größenwahn starb.

Einer Familie und dem Morgen entrissen,
Zuvor gestorben, danach nicht gelebt,
Durftest Du nie von der Zukunft wissen,
Die uns nach hundert Jahren noch bewegt,
Haben wir ohne Dich weiterleben müssen.

Mit Champagner, an Deinem Grab,
Trink ich auf die Zeit die Dir gegeben
In der es auch noch Tränen vor Freude gab.
So stoß ich an, auf ein viel zu kurzes Leben;
„Auf Onkel Hermann, der in Frankreich starb!"

Lens-Sallaumines, Mai 2017

Zum Gedenken an Hermann Hofmeister

Fredys Weg

„Wo ist nur die Zeit geblieben?" oder „Weißt Du noch?" gehören zu den üblichen Floskeln wenn es darum geht, einen „alten" Kollegen in den Ruhestand zu entlassen. Ein neuer Lebensabschnitt beginnt mit dem Ende des Arbeitslebens und dem Beginn des Ruhestandes oder der Pensionierung. Nicht jeder freut sich über den Eintritt ins Rentenalter denn die Umstellung von Arbeitszeit auf wohlverdiente Freizeit fällt oft nicht leicht und stellt neue Herausforderungen. Eine oftmals liebgewonnene Routine wird eingetauscht gegen eine noch unbekannte Zukunft. Wer in den Ruhestand eintritt kann hoffentlich auf ein erfolgreiches und zufriedenes Arbeitsleben zurückblicken. Ein persönliches Geschenk als Anerkennung der Leistungen des frisch gebackenen Rentners und die Dankbarkeit der Kollegen für die vielen guten gemeinsamen Stunden können als ein begleitendes „Schön war's" dabei helfen, den Weg in den Lebensabend zu versüßen.

Fredys Weg

Nun ist die Zeit uns schnell vergangen
Und vieles war, was keiner sah.
Im Goldenen Käfig mitgefangen;
Sei's doch egal, ob falsch, ob wahr!

Die Pflicht hast Du Dir groß geschrieben,
Die Zeit geschätzt und nicht verlebt,
Vom Geist auch mal zu gern getrieben
Auf mancher Wolke hoch geschwebt!

Und ist das Heute nicht das Ende,
Ein jeder Anfang fängt von vorn' neu an,
Legst Du das Glück in Deine Hände,
Wirst Du zum Manne nach dem Mann!

Gesteckt hast Du Dir die großen Ziele,
Über heimische Grenzen weit hinaus.
Zurück hingegen lässt Du viele –
Die spenden zum Abschied Dir Applaus!

Luxemburg, Januar 2016

The girl opposite...

...I didn't know her, I never talked to her.
I saw her through the window,
She was always there,
The girl opposite from across the street.
Sitting at her table, having breakfast;
She was my early-morning-coffee-constant.

Then, on a day in December,
The windows taped, the shutters down,
The girl opposite has moved!
I didn't know her, I never talked to her,
Yet, I just feel so abandoned.
How could she have done that to me,
The girl opposite from across the street?

Trier, December 2017

Little girl in a pub (being a parent)

Priorities shift but you come to realize that you gain so much more
without really having to give up too much of yourself.

...

Letztendlich ruft einen doch die Verantwortung. Die Prioritäten verschieben
sich, ohne dass man wirklich etwas aufgeben muss, von selbst, ist der Zuge-
winn doch ungleich größer.

from *"A Philosophy of Dreams"* (2009)

Little girl in a pub

Little girl in a pub, on a stool, at the bar,
Unpassionately bored,
Abandoned, like a little dog,
Sitting and waiting, trying to be quiet,
Making herself smaller,
"Sorry I'm around"!
While parents are drinking.

She catches my look, reads my concern,
Returns it with a tiny smile
And a glimpse of life in her eyes
– Too short –
Then a vacuous look returns to her face.
After some time: "Soon, soon, just be quiet!"
– No soon –
Poor little girl in a pub, on a stool, at the bar!

Trier, January 2018

Zwei kleine Geschichten / Two little Stories

Govi, the Elephant who wanted to be different

Long ago, there was a large herd of elephants that lived somewhere in the deep Indian jungle. The head elephant was the aged but very wise, Goshan. He had been able to call this herd his for many years, and over the course of these years, he learned a great deal. Almost nothing could surprise him anymore. Recently, however, the old female, Neela, had given birth, as a surprise to everybody, once again to a baby, and since then there had seemed to be some unrest among the members of the herd. Neela had named her small son Govi, meaning Curious. Govi lived up to his name entirely. He would always prowl around in the dangerous jungle alone and Neela could not keep up because of her age. He would constantly ask the other elephants questions like, 'Why is the sunshine gold?' or 'Why doesn't the rain have any colour?'. The members of the herd would just shake their heads, probably because they did not know. For several days, he had wanted to know why all elephants look alike and are grey. 'Elephants are grey, light grey, or dark grey, but in any case, always grey.' Goshan had answered him. However, Govi did not want to be like the other elephants, so Goshan's answer did not satisfy him. So he then asked the sun, whose golden rays were reflected in the river: 'Tell me, sun, why can't I be the same golden colour as you?'. The sun didn't give him an answer, so he asked the rain, which could find its way through the thick layers of the jungle: 'Tell me, rain, why can't I have no colour, just like you?' However, the rain did not give him an answer. This went on for days and weeks, until finally one night a Dream felt sorry for him and told him: 'Go, go to the plant with the large red flowers, eat from them every day and then wait.' Govi woke up the next morning, drank some of his old mother's milk, and went into the jungle. He soon found the plant with the large red flowers, just as had been mentioned in his dream. He quickly picked the biggest flower carefully and ate it when he heard Goshan say: 'Elephants don't eat big red flowers from plants! When you're older, you'll eat the young branches from the tops of the acacias, the fresh bark from the trees, or the juicy roots of the plants.' 'Why?' Govi then asked. 'Because that's how it's always been!' Goshan answered firmly. 'I think that's dumb!' Govi answered impudently, shaking his head and trumpeting, Goshan went away, shaking his head. For the next few weeks, Govi ate of the generous plant's large red flowers every morning – and the plant did not mind!

After some time, Govi noticed that the other elephants were whispering about him secretly. Even his old mother Neela seemed to have changed. 'Govi, where is your beautiful grey elephant colour?', she asked him. Govi looked at her, surprised, and the other elephants started to trumpet loudly with laughter. He ran quickly to the river, where the sun's golden rays were reflecting in the millions of colourless raindrops flowing by, and found that his reflection had turned pink. Overjoyed by no longer being grey, he thanked the river, which continued to flow without paying any attention to him.

In his short life, Govi had never been happier, but in her long life, his mother had never been sadder. Govi told each elephant in the herd about his dream, the dream that had made him different from all the other elephants in the entire world. Nevertheless, the other elephant children did not want to play with Govi anymore.

Grey elephant children do not play with pink elephant children. Elephant children only play with grey, light grey or dark grey elephants, but in any case, only with grey elephants. Thus, a few weeks went by and Govi grew very sad, until a dream took pity on him and said to him: 'Govi, go to the river, in which the sun's golden rays are reflecting in the millions of colourless raindrops flowing by, and drink water only from it and then wait.'
Govi went to the river the next morning and drank and he drank from the river for the next days and weeks.
'The rays of the sun are golden because they are golden, and the raindrops don't have any colour because they don't have any colour. Elephants are grey because they are grey', he heard Goshan saying loudly from behind him. 'Each species is unique in this world and it doesn't need any different colour to be better than or different from the others. Really being different is being yourself and that comes from the inside', he said, and tapped himself on the head with his trunk. 'And of what colour is the inside?' asked Govi, as he looked joyfully at his grey reflection in the river – but the river did not pay him any attention! a.v.i.s.

Epilogue
And the moon? Where in this story is the moon?
Dear reader, whenever you see the full moon, look up into the night - no, no, look much, much closer! Can you see his face? Well, the moon doesn't mind!

Good night stories

At the dusk of the day,
By early stars magic sparkle,
From the far Milky Way,
Old stories still circle!

Luxembourg, Isle of Man, Trier, 2002, 2017

The not-so-little-story of Mr Puss

"I walk like I talk and I talk like I walk; miaoouuuw!"

Let me introduce myself, my dear reader. They named me Mr Puss, or Mr P., as they oddly sometimes call me too. Not that I had anything to do with the choice of the name, it just happens to be Their choice. Who are They? Well, They consider themselves being my Masters. Often though, the female one refers to herself as „Mummy." Good golly, what has gone wrong?

Nevertheless, let's continue with my characteristics: my name is Mr Puss (bah, humbug!), with some many good years of age, all wrapped and packed in shiny black hair, except a small white spot on my chest, and last but not least, I'm a "Manxie". You have not heard of a Manxie? Dear me, what are you like? I come from the Isle of Man, the wee Island in the midst of the Irish Sea, where seagulls come in the size of Eagles, sheep carry four horns and cats have no tail. Yes, you heard right, cats have no tail and nor have I! You don't believe me, eh? As much as pigs cannot fly, does my island exist and - I have no tail!

Well, one day I travelled with my folks, led by a foreign star, across the dales, the seas and the mountains, all the way from my tiny Isle in the midst of the Irish Sea to the little land of Luxembourg, in the heart of Europe, my new going-to-be home. Cats have tails there! Long, warm summers and cold, snowy winters were to replace the Islands wind, mist and rain.

It was so much fun in the summer to laze about somewhere on the garden pathways and having the sun play tricks with my black fur, making it sparkle ginger and warming up my old bones with its rays. Purr!

❄ The winter painted my new world all white with some strange, cold stuff They called snow. Gosh, it made me follow my own paw's deep impressions around the garden thinking there were two of us:

"As there is no two of me, is there no two of thee!"

It is so enjoyable having the extreme seasons and changing my coat from summer to winter and the other way around and leaving balls of fur everywhere around the house for Them. Uhm, also I'm not too sure of the Their appreciation?!

Dear me, sometimes I seem to also upset Them, sharpening my claws on some of Their weird stuff around or even scratching my "Mummy's" eye, trying to finally wake her up in the morning: "Miaow, hey, breakfast!" How can one forget about breakfast?

🖼 I just love my home and I am so happy and glad that They look after me, purr, puurr! But one day -miaow!!- another, almost like me, came into MY home! They called him Treacle and he was a tailed one! Of all cats, a tailed one! From then on, suddenly, I had to share my life with this tailed, longhaired, black rascal.

"Never expect the Now as the certain and never take things for granted!"

I managed slowly to get used to the other other-one but me-one in the house. I usually went my way and He went his. The occasional competition for food was tolerable and finding an own place to sleep and laze was no problem as there are plenty of beds in the house. He did not challenge me over my window ledge and sofa cushion and eventually we even managed to get on together by some sort of positive feline ignorance.

🎄 Now and then, when there was plenty of white stuff about, They brought some of the outside to the inside; a tree appeared in the house with plenty of things put on and under. They were particular cuddly and friendly at that time and there was plenty more to eat for me and the tailed-one. We both love chicken, miouw! Life has once again become so cosy and happy, as if it has brought heaven to earth for me; it's just so purr, puurr, puuurr! And why am I telling you all of this?

Well, I'm a cat with no hat,
A puss with no boots,
Don't come from Bremen nor Cheshire,
But I am Mr Puss
Or Mr P. – as they oddly sometimes call me!

I'd like to finish my not-so-little-story here now, but don't forget, … I'm a very tired little black cat with no tail, with some many good years of age, all the way from the Isle of Man, and…

One day, when I die,
You know, I'm not far.
Please, do not cry,
I'm always your star,
Just look at the sky!

In memory of "Mr P., that is he" for "Julie, that is she".

Trier, Luxembourg, Christmas 2015

Über Orte / About Places

Earl Grey

It is here – in midst of the Irish Sea,
Where seagulls circle in the size of eagles,
The prowling cats have no tail,
The grazing Loaghtan bears the weight of his four horns
And the little people under the bridge demanding a Hello!

Fading in the early morning's mist in my Victorian garden,
Drinking Earl Grey with its Bergamot scent from within,
Surrounded by the Island's salty air
And spicy oriental flavours in my mind.

Still – in all shades of blue the sea is coming in,
And, above, white cottages in midst of green painted hills
With dabs of gorse's, yellow and heather's purple.

Time enough is "Traa-dy-Liooar"
Time enough – it is here!

Luxembourg, February 2016

Reichensteiner

When I went to the local Inn tonight,
In olde Bradford-on-Avon,
The waiter offered full of pride
His local wine of "Deutsche Reben".

I looked at him and asked surprised:
"Your German Wine is from these soils?"
He replied to me all undisguised:
"Oh yes, indeed, of sweat and toils!"

"After many years we did succeed
To grow the wine in our yards-
But it's English now and not too sweet,
All making it by our hearts!"

Bradford-on-Avon, 2013

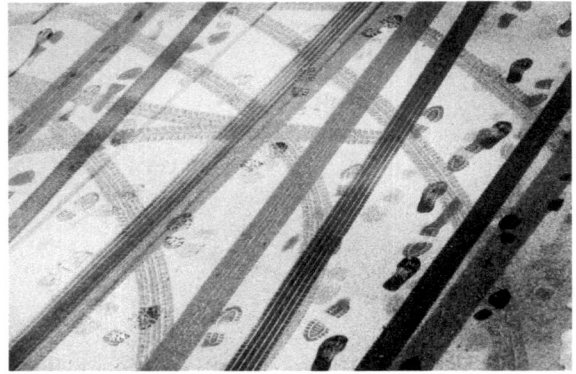

Trier

Looking out of the window,
Watching people going by,
Leaving footprints in fresh snow;
Why don't I?

Trier, March 2013

Pizza Hut

Prowling around town, looking for food,
Like some lonely wolf.
None of my usual bourgeois larders seem tempting enough tonight for calling in;
Ending up at Pizza Hut!

Uli Krentz, October, 2017

Kleine Konditorei

Die Türe für immer geschlossen,
Die Auslagen bleiben leer,
Mein Tisch von gestern steht heute verlassen;
Des Meisters Torten verführen nie mehr!

Der Zeit entflohen bin ich hier,
Ließ draußen zurück den Lärm der Welt.
Von feinstem Gebäck bestellt' ich mir;
Das kleine Glück für wenig Geld!

So schau ich nur die Mauern von Tradition
Und weiß sogleich es ist nicht mehr,
Sehn' ich mir in Gedanken schon
Hier einen neuen Zuckerbäcker her!

Trier, 2016

Karl Marx Statue

In Erinnerung an den 200. Geburtstag des Philosophen Karl Marx wurde in der Trierer Innenstadt ein wahrlich großes Geschenk Chinas für den großen Sohn der Stadt aufgestellt: Die Karl-Marx-Statue, die China der Stadt Trier als Geburtsstadt des Philosophen zum Jubiläumsjahr 2018 geschenkt hat. Angefertigt hat das Kunstwerk der über die chinesischen Grenzen hinaus bekannte Bildhauer Wu Weishan.
Der Trierer Stadtrat hat sich anfänglich mit dem großzügigen Geschenk aus dem Reich der Mitte sehr schwer getan, und man einigte sich schließlich auf eine etwas geringere Höhe der Skulptur von immer noch 5,50m.

Karl Marx Statue

In memory of the 200th birthday of the philosopher Karl Marx, a truly great gift of China for the city's great son was erected in Trier's city centre: The Karl Marx statue, which China donated to the city of Trier as the birthplace of the philosopher for the 2018 anniversary year. The work of art has been produced by the international well-known Chinese sculptor Wu Weishan,
The city council of Trier was initially struggling with the generous gift from the Middle Kingdom and finally agreed to a slightly lower height of the sculpture, still standing at 5.50m.

Karl Marx, geschenkt!

Zurückgekommen ist er in seine alte Stadt,
- Philosoph, Weltveränderer und Kommunist -
Auf einen Sockel hat man ihn gehoben
Und ihn in Form gebracht, aus edlem Metall,
Ausgeliefert schaut er übergroß herab,
Einem Patrizier gleich,
Inmitten 2000 Jahre alter Ruinen.
Von weit her angereist, aus dem Reich der Mitte,
Erreicht er der Proletarier Kinder kaum mehr.

Besucher aus neuer, materieller Heimat
Tragen in Mandarin sein Kapital umher.
Mit bourgeoisem Smartphone bewaffnet
Kommen seine fast zahllosen Schwärmer.
Kann von hier nicht fliehen in ein Exil;
Gefangen im hohlen, starren Korpus.
Zu schwer für Engels Flügel,
Nur unweit des Schwarzen Tores, harrend,
Von Westphalen träumend - Sie wird nicht kommen!

Trier, 2017

Stolperstein

Die Stolpersteine sind ein Projekt des Künstlers Gunter Demnig aus Berlin, das im Jahr 1992 begann. Mit im Boden verlegten kleinen Gedenktafeln soll an das Schicksal der Menschen erinnert werden, die in der Zeit des Nationalsozialismus verfolgt, ermordet, deportiert, vertrieben oder in den Suizid getrieben wurden. Diese, dem Kopfsteinpflaster nachempfundenen Messingquadrate sind mit von Hand eingeschlagenen Lettern beschriftet und werden von einem angegossenen Betonwürfel getragen. Sie werden, da wo möglich, vor den letzten Wohnhäusern der NS-Opfer niveaugleich in das Pflaster oder den Belag des jeweiligen Gehwegs eingelassen. Ungefähr 61000 Steine sind zurzeit verlegt und das nicht nur in Deutschland, sondern auch in 21 weiteren europäischen Ländern. Die Stolpersteine gelten als das größte dezentrale Mahnmal der Welt.

Stolpertstein

A "Stolperstein" or in English a "trip stone" or "stumbling block" is a monument or memorial created by the German artist Gunter Demnig from Berlin, to commemorate a victim of Nazi oppression, including the Holocaust. Stolpersteine are small, cobblestone-sized memorials made of brass for an individual victim of Nazism usually placed at the location where he/she once lived. They commemorate individuals, both, those who died and survivors – who were consigned by the Nazis to prisons, euthanasia facilities, sterilization clinics, concentration camps, and extermination camps, as well as those who responded to persecution by emigrating or committing suicide. About 61,000 so far being placed in 21 countries and it is considered the world largest memorial.

Stolperstein

Wenn ich durch Triers Straßen geh',
Nehmen Häuser mich mit durch die Zeit
Und bisweilen in deren Fenster seh';
Stumme Mauern mit verhalltem Leid.

Den schönen Stuck schau ich gern mir an,
Da, wo er die Fassaden auch heut noch ziert,
Ziehen mich Geschichten in ihren Bann,
Tief in gelbgoldenes Messing eingraviert.

Aus Epochen von über zweitausend Jahren
Steht Bauwerk noch immer prunkvoll da
Und auch in neuem Glanz von frischen Farben,
Hält es ein Stück vergessene Geschichte wahr.

Das Kopfsteinpflaster funkelt seine Narben
Vor so mancher Brache oder Haus,
Erinnert an die Besitzer die gelebt hier haben,
Zu der Zeit von Pogrom und Holocaust.

Bürger wurden ermordet und vertrieben,
Lebten unter Gleichen in dieser Stadt.
Doch nur die Häuser sind heut noch geblieben,
Dessen Bewohner man längst vergessen hat!

„Name ist Schall und Rauch"
So kommt es schon im "Faust" daher,
Doch – ein Mensch ist eben Name auch,
Erst ohne Name ist der Mensch nicht mehr!

„Wirklich tot ist ein Mensch erst dann,
Wenn keiner sich erinnern kann!"

Uli Krentz, Trier/Luxemburg, Juni 2015

Cubiculum

So manchen Nächten hab' ich hier nachgeweint
Und steig' darum auch heut hinab die vielen Stufen.
Kein Licht der Stadt durchs Fenster scheint
Und klingt hinaus auch nicht berauschtes Rufen.

Von alten Schaukästen trink ich mein Bier,
Nur die jungen Gesichter sind so spät noch verblieben
Und des einst Tabaks Rauch, so scheint es mir,
Ist wohl nun in meinen Whisky vertrieben.

Der währende Augenblick bleibt mir neu geboren.
Vor lautem Gerede, bleib ich gerne stumm.
Stunden vergehen und sind doch nie verloren,
In Triers Altstadt am Morgen - im Cubiculum.

Luxemburg/Trier, November 2014

Brunnenmeister von Weimar

Frühmorgens, die Stadt scheint verschlafen und verlassen,
Als träumt' sie von deutscher Geschichte und altem Grandeur,
Da stört ein Motorengeräusch den Frieden der Gassen;
Im Gefährt, ganz amtlich mit Auftrag, Herr Ingenieur,
Soll die städtischen Brunnen der Zeiten Zahn nicht überlassen.

An heißen Sommertagen oder bei Herbstes rauen Winden
Den Goethebrunnen, am Frauenplan, von Blättern befreien
Und auch bei klirrender Kälte Fehler und Lösungen finden
Und beim ‚Spucken und Schlucken' die Ventile erneuern.

Umspielt das Wasser auch die verschiedensten Gestalten,
Dem Meister vom Handwerk, dem darf man wohl glauben;
Die urbanen Quellen immer fließen, meisterlich erhalten!

Weimar/Trier/Luxemburg, Mai/Juli 2015

Andere so Sachen / Other such Things

Ach, Mensch!

Wird der Mensch doch niemals weise,
Sucht stets den eigenen Vorteil nur,
Wähnt sich allein auf seiner Reise,
Sieht nur sich selbst auf weiter Flur!

Doch zum Lernen braucht es Lehrer,
Für neues Leben immer zwei,
Alleine wiegt das Leben schwerer,
Gemeinsam ist der Mensch erst frei!

Luxemburg/Trier 2016

Ich bin!
Bin ich?

...mich

Es ist die Stille, die mich träumen lässt,
mit all ihren Geräuschen!

Es ist die Angst, die mich machen lässt,
mit all ihren Kräften!

Es ist der Zweifel, der mich hoffen lässt,
mit all seinen Mitteln!

Es ist die Liebe, die mich hassen lässt,
mit all ihrer Nähe!

...ich, Trier, Mai 2016

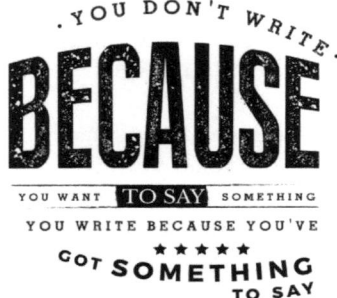

Mein (Nicht-)Reimgedicht

Dies ist mein Gedicht - das sich nicht reimt,
Nicht nach der zweiten Zeile
Und auch nicht nach der Dritten!
So fällt es schwer mir diese Vierte zu verfassen,
Und nach der fünften Zeile dann,
Kann ich's in der Sechsten doch nicht lassen!

Trier, August 2013

Cyber Poet

Going through my thoughts of the day;
Sitting in front of the screen,
Playing with the words,
Adding and deleting,
Copying and pasting,
Making lines fit,
Completing them to verses.
Sometimes it works,
Sharing in social media.
Often it doesn't!

Trier, November 2017

"There's no place like home,
there's no place like home,
there's no place like home!"

Dorothy Gale (from Kansas)

Gastfreundschaft

Mein Teil von Trier,
Ein kleines Stück Welt,
Bin hier ich Zuhause,
Hab' neu mich bestellt!

…und sind meine Gäste auch verschieden,
Der gute Geschmack sie doch vereint.
Und denen, die spät noch geblieben,
Das Licht am wärmsten scheint!

Trier, September 2013

Insomnia

Cor, me!
To the ones who can't sleep at night;
"The snows of Kilimanjaro" lies like a hard crust on me -
And
Dreaming, within the dream, of Death Valley's immane heat,
Evaporating my last active sleep hormones left for this night to be!
Who cares?

Trier, 2017

Draußen...

Die Platzangst treibt mich
Nach einer zu langen Nacht,
Im Bett - hält mich gefangen.

Die Decke fällt mir auf den Kopf,
Ich möchte nur noch raus!
Ich schau' aus dem Fenster,
Die Stadt schläft noch.

Späte Nachtschwärmer auf dem Weg nach Hause -
Ich möchte nur noch raus!
Und bleib ich doch lieber in meinen vier Wänden
Fernab von – zu viel Raum und zu viel Mensch.

Ich bin selbst mein Kosmos,
Lichtjahre von dem da draußen entfernt.
Die Decke fällt mir auf den Kopf,
Ich möchte nur noch raus!

Ich schau aus dem Fenster
Und möchte nur noch raus
Und - bleibe doch lieber
In meinen vier Wänden…

…ist es auch nicht anders!

Trier/Isle of Man 2017

Kinder-Nachtmahr

„Papa, ich habe Angst vorm Sterben!"
„Ach, mein Kind, Angst kommt und geht
Und selbst der Tod, wenn er dann letztendlich kommt,
Bleibt nur eine Sekunde!"

Douglas, Isle of Man, September 2017

...

Child-Nightmare

"Daddy, I'm scared of death!"
"Oh, my dear, fear comes and goes
And even Death, when he finally comes by,
Will only stay for one second!"

Douglas, Isle of Man, September 2017

Seelenverkäufer

Unter dem Begriff Boatpeople versteht man ursprünglich die in der Folge des Vietnamkrieges in Südostasien geflohenen Menschen, zumeist vietnamesischer Herkunft. Heute wird er auch für nahezu alle Menschen verwendet, die in Booten fliehen. Internationale Schlepperorganisationen vermitteln für horrende Summen Plätze auf solchen Booten. Solche Fluchten werden meist mit ungeeigneten und zudem überladenen und nur bedingt schwimmbaren „Seelenverkäufern" versucht. Die Ursachen von Bootsflucht reichen heute, wie bei jeder Flucht, von individueller über religiöser Verfolgung und bewaffneter Konflikte bis hin zur Suche nach wirtschaftlich und klimatisch besseren Lebensbedingungen.

"Seelenverkäufer"

The term boatpeople is originally associated with the people who fled Southeast Asia as a result of the Vietnam War, mostly of Vietnamese origin. Today it is also used for almost all people fleeing in boats. International human traffickers organizations sell places on such boats for horrendous sums of money. Such escapes are usually attempted with unsuitable and also overloaded "floating coffins" ("Seelenverkäufer"). The causes of fleeing by boat today, as with every flight, range from individual and religious persecution, armed conflicts and to the search for economic and climatic better living conditions.

Seelenverkäufer

Wenn Panik tiefe Furchen ins Gesicht sich gräbt,
Kinder vor Angst immer noch lauter schreien,
Das Meer das alte Boot nur noch irgendwie trägt
Auf Wellen – halten gefangen – und sollten doch befreien.

Ganz andere Menschen, alle gleich verzweifelt blicken,
Zusammengepfercht, zu Hundert, auf kleinstem Raum.
Größer nur mehr das Grauen leben, größer die Sorgen drücken;
Ohne zu schlafen aufzuwachen, in bösem Traum!

Alles verloren, das liegt zurück – nach vorne nichts gewonnen;
Das Meer, das fordert ständig Tribut
Hat so manches Leben sich schon genommen
Aus dieser steten Menschenflut!

Luxemburg/Trier 2016

Zeitenwende

Hab' immer schon an Dich gedacht
Seit wir uns einst zum Cocktail trafen
Und haben wir auch viel gelacht,
Sollt' in jener Nacht allein ich schlafen.

Die Zeit, sie hat ihr Spiel geschrieben
Mit Regeln kaum von mir gemacht.
Hab' diese ich nun selbst geschrieben,
Bin endlich mit Dir aufgewacht!

Und denk auch gern ich an die Jahre
Als ich geliebt hab' tief im Herzen,
Bist Du doch heut' die wirklich wahre;
Vergessen sind die alten Schmerzen.

So spielen für mich nun tausend Geigen
Und kein Vorhang der je fällt.
Möcht' ich die Liebe gern nun zeigen
Auf allen Bühnen dieser Welt.

Bin ich auch wach, ist's wie im Traume,
Kommt doch das Gestern heut' zu mir
Und find ich mich in weitem Raume,
Tanz ich den Tango nur mit Dir!

Luxemburg, August 1986, Oktober 2010

Erwachen

Wenn sich frühmorgens meine Lider heben
Und noch schönste Gedanken um mich schweben,
Fühl ich mich wohl in meiner Haut;
Hab' gerne meinen Träumen nachgeschaut!

Luxemburg, November 2010

Der Hahn

Der Hahn, der kräht
Im Morgengrauen.
Den Wind, der weht,
Hat's umgehauen!

Die Hühner fragen:
- Der Hahn der hustet -
„Wer soll's ihm sagen?"
Der Hahn, der pustet!

Da kommt der Bauer:
- Das Beil zur Hand -
„Die Milch ist sauer"!
Der Hahn verschwand!

Die Hühner klagen
- Der Bauer frohlockt -
„Wer soll's ihm sagen?"
Die Stimmung stockt!

Die Sonne geht auf,
Die Sonne geht unter.
Die Hühner, Leiter ,rauf,
Die Hühner, Leiter runter!

Kein Hahn, der kräht.
Der Bauer singt!
Der Wind verwehts,
Weil's krähend klingt!

Der Hahn, der kräht,
- Man glaubt es nicht -
Ist wieder da,
Nahm Unterricht!

Der Bauer ist heiser,
Die Hühner am Ziele,
- Ein Jeder ist weiser -
Und Eier ganz viele!

Trier, April 2017

Paddy's Day

You pay for my Whiskey
And I'll write ya a poem.
You make it a Second
And I'll give it a tune.
Let's finish on Third,
And I'll dance ya the moon!

Luxembourg, March 2016

2:41 pm (Vitso's Poem)

After a morning filled with gloom,
The sun arrives to brighten my day,
Tired of skiving, shining in somebody else's room:
"I'll come and go as it pleases my way!"

Trier/Luxembourg, March /September 2016

Über-Leben

Das größte im Leben ist der Tod,
Wir leben täglich darauf hin –
Und kommt er schließlich dann,
Verbleibt er nur für einen Herzschlag!

Isle of Man, 2015

...

Outlive

The biggest thing in life is death
And every day this thought we greet
And when finally he comes along,
He stays just for one heart beat!

Isle of Man, 2015

Ewiger Cowboy

Wenn dann im Grab ich endlich ruh',
Wünscht' ich es käm' ein Reitermann,
-Mit breitem Hut und spitzen Stiefeln-
Der hört' mein' stummen Rufen zu,
Die sonst der Wind nur hören kann:

„Pflanz Du ein kleines Bäumchen mir,
Und wächst's auch noch in tausend Jahren,
-Singst Du das ew'ge Lied für mich-
Erzählt ein jedes Blatt nur Dir
Geschichten wie sie einst mal waren."

Luxemburg, 2015

Eternal Cowboy

When in my grave I finally lie,
I wish a horseman would come by;
-With a wide brim hat and pointed boots-
Who listens to my silent calls
Heard only by the wind so high:

„Go plant a tree down in my vale,
To grow for a thousand years
-You sing the eternal song I loved-
Each of its leaves tells you a tale
About my past, for those with ears!"

Luxembourg, 2015

Zu diesem Gedicht
Gibt es keinen Reim;
Was sich mir damals
Schon nicht reimte,
Wird dies heute
Auch nicht tun.
Zu diesem Gedicht
Gibt es kein Bild;
Kein Bild kann
Der Opfer je
Gerecht werden!

Deutscher Herbst

Und immer dann, wenn ich keine Worte finde, ich ein Gedicht schreibe!

Die surreale Emergenz des Terrorismus als ein zutiefst prägender Teil deutscher Nachkriegszeitgeschichte ist bis heute bei mir und vielen meiner Generation präsent, nur allzu allgegenwärtig...

...der „Deutsch Herbst" hat mich schon als pubertierender Bub verändert bevor ich überhaupt war - zu schnell Winter werdend und zu lang auf den Frühling wartend!

Steckbriefe mit ihrer rotgerahmten Omnipräsenz in Postämtern, Sparkassen und Behörden projizieren mir bis heute die hässlichen Bilder der Siebziger.
Landshut, Mogadishu, Stammheim;
Kein Pflaster, kein Verband der diese Wunden je heilen wird.
All dieses ausgelöst von den Tätern nach den Tätern! Und, ja, das Leben geht weiter - nur eben anders!

Keine Namen, nicht die der Opfer, nicht die der Täter!

Trier/Luxemburg/Isle of Man, 2016/17

Aufsatz über meinen Geburtstag / Essay on my Birthday

Ich habe Geburtstag! (Ein kleiner Aufsatz über meinen Geburtstag)

Ach ja, nun ist es wieder so weit; es ist mein Geburtstag! Und ja, in der Tat, es ist immer noch ein spezieller Tag für mich und das war er auch immer schon! Eine für mich mittlerweile fast undenkbar groß scheinende Zahl von Lebensjahren fordert meine äußerst begrenzten mathematischen Fähigkeiten immer mehr bis auf das Äußerste heraus! Geburtstage waren immer schon von besonderer emotionaler, fast spiritueller Bedeutung für mich, auch Dank meiner Mutter!

Vor sehr langer Zeit, als ich ein kleiner Junge war, gestaltete meine Mutter, entgegen aller wirtschaftlichen oder gar gesundheitlichen Schwierigkeiten, an diesem Tag immer etwas Besonderes, ja fast magisches. Wieder, wenn im familiären Terminkalender Geburtstag stand, lief das gleiche Prozedere ab; ein schön eingedeckter Geburtstagstisch im Esszimmer mit wunderbar verpackten Geschenken. Diese bestanden immer aus einer gesunden Mischung von Kleidung ("Zeug") und Spielzeug. Mitten auf dem Tisch war oftmals eine Torte, ganz nach dem Geschmack des Jubilars, platziert. In meinem Fall war das meistens, saisonbedingt, ein Erdbeerkuchen oder auch meine Lieblingstorte Schwarzwälder Kirsch. Ich hatte immer Schwierigkeiten am Abend vorher Schlaf zu finden, war die Vorfreude doch so überwältigend. Selbst die vier Nichtgeburtstagsbrüder sollten, war der Morgen gekommen, nicht vergessen werden, wurden sie doch mit passenden Aufmerksamkeiten zum "kleinen Geburtstag" bedacht. Erst nach einem "Uli hat Geburtstag" Ständchen durften die zahlreichen Geschenke ausgepackt werden. Ich liebe Geburtstag – und ich wünschte mir, dass all die anderen 19.300.000 (neunzehn Millionen dreihunderttausend) Menschen auf dieser Welt, die diesen Tag mit mir teilen, ähnliches Glück finden würden! Herzliche Glückwünsche zum Geburtstag, Euch allen!

Trier/Isle of Man, 28. Juni 2011

It's my Birthday! (A little Essay on my Birthday)

Well, here I am again; it is my birthday! Moreover, it is a very special day to me, and it always has been! In addition, considering my absolute mathematical incapability, for me an almost literally unthinkable number of years to follow!

Birthdays are and always have been, very special, almost spiritual, meaningful and emotional to me. Mostly thanks to my mother!

A very long time ago when I was little, and it came around again, she always made it, despite ill health or lack of money, a one and only special, almost magical day for my brothers and I. There's always been a birthday-table ready for us in the early morning of our annual jubilee. Our dining table, all beautifully decorated and filled with amazingly well wrapped presents, decorations and home-baked birthday cake has always been the cause of sleepless nights before. The always-present cake was exclusively chosen to the current birthday boy's preference and taste, in my case the seasonable Strawberry Cake or the classic Black-Forest-Gateau. One always had difficulties falling asleep the night before! And, to make sure that nobody felt left out, the four "none-birthday-brothers" were also always presented some "littlebirthday-present" as a memento for the day. To complete a true Happy-Birthday-Boys Dream, everybody around the table chanted 'Happy Birthday to you' (German version though)! I just love Birthdays and I'd wish (and unfortunately know I'm still dreaming) that the other Nineteen-million-three-hundred-thousand (19.300.000) people sharing this same day would also be able to have such a good time! Happy Birthday to you all!

Trier/Isle of Man, 28 June 2011

Übersetzungen / Translations

„C'est un amour..."

„C'est un amour qui contient dieu, les anges et la nature immense. C'est un amour vient de loin. Il vient du fond d'une solitude sans fond et de plus loin encore, du savoir d'une jouissance sans déclin. Il n'y a pas d'autre amour que cet amour de loin. Il n'y a qu'un seul amour comme on dit: une seule loi, la même absence dans la souffrance comme dans la joie. Ce qu'on apprend dans les livres, c'est-à-dire, ‚je vous aime'.»

Christian Bobin - 1999 - La part manquante

...

„Es ist eine Liebe..."

„Es ist eine Liebe, die Gott, die Engel und die unermessliche Natur enthält. Es ist eine Liebe, die aus der Ferne kommt. Sie kommt aus dem Grund einer bodenlosen Einsamkeit und darüber hinaus, aus dem Wissen eines Genusses ohne Verfall. Es gibt keine andere Liebe als diese Liebe aus der Ferne. Es gibt nur eine Liebe, wie man sagt: Ein einziges Gesetz, das gleiche Fehlen im Leid wie in der Freud'. Das ist es was man aus den Büchern lernt, das heißt: ‚Ich liebe Dich'."

Christian Bobin - 1999 - La part manquante

...

"It's a love..."

"It's a love which contains God, the angels and immeasurable nature. It's a love, which comes from afar. It comes from a bottomless loneliness and more than that, of knowing about enjoyment without end. There is no other love than this love from afar. There is only one love as they say: a single law, the same absence in suffering as in joy. It is what one learns from books, meaning: ‚I love you'."

Christian Bobin - 1999 - La part manquante

Der Tod ist groß...

Der Tod ist groß.
Wir sind die Seinen
lachenden Munds.
Wenn wir uns mitten im Leben meinen,
wagt er zu weinen
mitten in uns.

Rainer Maria Rilke, aus: Das Buch der Bilder

...

Death is great...

Death is great,
We are his –
Laughing mouths
When we see ourselves in the midst of life,
Dare he to cry
In the midst of us.

.....

"The dead are not so very far away.
They're just... on the other side of the wall.
It's us, on this side, who are, all of us, so... alone!"

From "Mr Holmes", BBC Films

...

„Die Toten sind gar nicht so weit entfernt,
sie sind nur... auf der anderen Seite der Wand.
Es sind wir, die auf dieser Seite so... alleine sind!"

Aus "Mr. Holmes", BBC Films

Halloween

Halloween n'a rien de drôle. Ce Festival sarcastique reflète plutôt une soif de revanche des enfants sur le monde adulte.

Jean Baudrillard

...

Halloween

Es ist nichts lustiges an Halloween, dieses boshafte Fest spiegelt vielmehr der Kinder teuflisches Bedürfnis nach Rache an der Welt der Erwachsenen wieder.

Jean Baudrillard

...

Halloween

There is nothing funny about Halloween. This sarcastic festival reflects rather an infernal demand for revenge by children on the adult world.

Jean Baudrilliard

Aphorismen - Aphorisms

Although one cannot live in the past,
one still needs to live with its consequences!

Auch wenn man nicht in der Vergangenheit leben kann
muss man doch mit ihren Konsequenzen leben!

...

Stupidity is not to expect the obvious!

...

Just always, take one step after the other,
Pause in between –think– and continue walking!

...

When telling a story, never mind false or true, do it with your heart!

...

Der Krieg ist die hässliche Fratze der Menschheit!

War is the ugly face of humankind!

...

Was Oma noch wusste weiß heute das Internet.

...

Kann man den Tod auch nicht verstehen
Und will man vom Sterben nichts wissen
Sollte man das Leben doch kennen!

KRENTZ

Auch nach den schlimmsten Fehlern geht es trotzdem weiter,
nur anders!

Even after the worst mistakes, life still goes on- but different!

...

Es gibt die Welt so oft wie diese Menschen hat!

The world exists as often as there are people!

...

Es gibt Momente die einem gleich als solche scheinen!

There are moments, which instantly appear to one as such!

...

Lässt sich Freundschaft auch nach der Länge der Zeit bemessen,
Misst sie sich vor allen Dingen aber nach der Größe des Herzens!

Does friendship also depend on the length of its time,
It is above all the size of its heart that counts!

Epice*logue*

Indian Hybrid Curry Dish "Poetry of Scents and Flavours"

One can find absolute everything about life in an Indian Curry. It is a true spiritual experience to spend some time together with your partner, family or friends preparing a meal of thousand-and-one scents. The m orning for such an event is the time for shopping, strolling across the local markets, visiting the Oriental shops and calling in to the neighbourhood butcher (there, where non-vegetarian) finding all the ingredients necessary for composing a culinary "Dance on the Tongue". Blending spices is like writing poetry; everything has to become a palatable rhyme! The Red and Yellow of the Rajasthan deserts, the fruity flavours and spicy scents of Goa and Kerala and the sizzling and steamy atmosphere of Mumbai's street kitchen; it is almost like being on a voyage through the sub-continent within your own four walls.

Shopping list (list of ingredients; four portions):

6 tablespoons of ghee (Olive or sunflower oil as some emergency alternative)
4-6 cloves
2-3 sticks of cinnamon
3 green cardamom pods
4-6 berries of Sansho Pepper (where available)
1-table spoon of cumin seeds
2 medium sized onion, chopped
2 table spoons of chopped ginger
4-6 cloves of garlic, chopped
½-tablespoon of ground turmeric
1½ tablespoon of curry powder
½-tablespoon of curcuma
½-tablespoon of ground coriander
½-tablespoon of Chilli powder
½-tablespoon of black pepper
6-8 dried Chillies
3-4 tomatoes, puréed, or 300 g of tinned, pulpy tomato sauce
1 tablespoon of spicy mustard

150 ml of natural yoghurt (or 100ml of crème fraîche if preferred)
250 g all-purpose potatoes (ca. 5)
200 g fresh Mango
600 g of free-range chicken filet
150-200 ml of water
1-tablespoon of garam masala[1]
1-handful of fresh coriander leaves
4 Mint leaves

Let's get started:
After you had, hopefully, a great morning out finding everything and ticking off your shopping list, you should prepare the various ingredients. A proper and well thought through preparation prior the actual cooking is the most important thing when it comes to cooking (e.g.: peeling, chopping, slicing, weighing etc.)!

First step:
Grind the 3-4 dried chillies, cloves, cardamom pods, Japanese Sansho pepper and cumin seeds in a mortar and pre-heat a small non-stick pan with three tablespoon of ghee. Add the ground spices, fry for about 30 seconds until aromatic, and put aside. Peel the Mango and potatoes. Chop the Mango to medium cubed size. Chop the 5 potatoes into 4 and boil in a separate pan for about 20 minutes.

Second step:
Give the chopped onions into the rest of the ghee (three tablespoons) into a large frying pan and cook for about 3 minutes until golden brown, occasionally stirring. Add the chicken and cook over at medium high heat for 4-5 minutes. Stir in the curcuma, ginger and garlic and cook stirring for about 1 minute before adding some pinches of salt and the ground spices (with the first three tablespoons of ghee) and stir again for about 1 minute. Pour in the tomatoes and cook over a medium heat for about 10-15 minutes, until the liquid in the pan has become saucy.

Meanwhile preparing Pilau Rice (but plain rice will do too!):

40 g butter
250ml basmati rice
1-teaspoon turmeric
1 bay leaf (if available)
4 green cardamom pods
4 cloves
½-teaspoon fennel seed
1-teaspoon salt
250ml boiling water

Melt the butter in a saucepan.
Stir in the rice until it is all coated in the butter.
Add the spices and salt.

Add the boiling water.
Cover with a tight fitting lid, and allow to simmer on a low heat for 15 minutes. No need to stir!

Third step:
Add enough water to half cover the chicken (about 150ml - 200ml), bring it to boil and then cook over a low heat until the chicken is cooked. Mix the mustard with the yoghurt and pour in together. Add the potatoes, two tablespoons of chopped coriander and the three cinnamon sticks and let simmer. The slower it cooks the better it tastes. This takes about 15 minutes for small pieces and up to 25-30 minutes for larger ones. Half way through the cooking add the Mango. After finished the cooking, serve in a bowl, decorate with the rest of chopped coriander and the recovered cinnamon sticks.

Fourth step:
Serve the Pilau rice and sprinkle with some Garam masala[1] and Indian flatbreads (chapatti or nan) and Raita[2] or any vegetable dish.

Garam masala[1] is a popular spice for adding to meat dishes to give an authentic Indian flavour. Literally translated, this means 'hot spices' and it is a blend of a number of roasted and finely ground spices that are designed to bring warmth and aroma. There is no definitive recipe for Garam masala, though traditionally it contains a basic mix of cloves, black pepper, cinnamon and cardamom. However, the amounts and extra-added spices vary from cook to cook and region to region in India with other flavourings such as fennel, cumin and coriander seeds, nutmeg, mace, bay leaves and chillies finding their way into the blend. Though many spices are fried at the beginning of cooking to bring out their unique taste – the special aroma of Garam masala can often be more effective when sprinkled on at the end, like a seasoning.

It can easily be bought ready mixed too, though the taste may have less depth of flavour and fragrance than if freshly ground and blended.

For your info:

Raita[2] recipe ingredients:

200 gr of natural yoghurt
100 gr of cucumber
2 tablespoons of milk
¼ tablespoon of salt
¼ tablespoon of garam masala (optional)
¼ tablespoon of chilli powder (optional)

Add all together and mix well! 4 Mint leaves for decoration (one for each portion), ready!

वोन अप्पेतित · Enjoy your meal! · Guten Appetit!

Curry Concert

It'll take a good while for preparing a curry,
Composing out of fragrant aromatic spices.
Indian cooking can't be done in a hurry;
Conducting a concert of thousand choices!

Trier/Isle of Man, September 2017

...und dann kommt, was kommen muß;
As moments fly,
Am Ende kommt dann doch der Schluß!
The time goes by!

Ende · The End